Titans of the

DEEP

Dr. Olivia Reed

Preface

I magine a world where a single heartbeat could echo through the expanse of an entire city block, a world where a single stride could span the length of a football field. Indeed, from the depths of the oceans to the heights of the skies, and the expanses of prehistoric landscapes, the giants have walked, swam, and soared.

The blue whale holds the crown as the largest creature to ever inhabit this planet. Yet, alongside this modern behemoth, we'll unearth the remnants of the megalodon, the apex predator of prehistory, and delve into the lives of ancient plesiosaurs and ichthyosaurs that once patrolled primeval oceans.

Colossal creatures, such as the towering sauropods, etched their stories into the rocks and soils, leaving behind awe-inspiring footprints for us to decipher. The story doesn't end there, as we explore the immense indricotherium, a land mammal that would dwarf even the most imposing modern-day elephants. And let's not forget the gargantuan insects that once shared our world, as massive as they were fascinating.

But the skies, too, have been home to giants. We'll spread our wings alongside the quetzalcoatlus, a pterosaur that soared with an elegance that belied its size. We'll glide alongside the albatross, a modern-day marvel of flight, and unravel the secrets of airborne giants that once graced ancient skies.

From the folklore and legends that weave tales of giants in our midst to the modern-day conservation efforts aimed at safeguarding the surviving giants, our story becomes intertwined with theirs.

We'll start with *uncovering the physics* that both enable and constrain their enormous dimensions, exploring how their metabolisms fuel these epic proportions. And as we ponder the evolutionary advantages and compromises that come with size, we'll peer into the future, speculating on the potential resurrection of extinct giants and the impact of changing climates on the grandest of inhabitants.

Evolutionary Forces

———

Picture, if you will, a primordial landscape teeming with life's pioneers. Here, amidst the struggle for sustenance and the chase for survival, a peculiar dynamic begins to take shape. When resources are abundant and competitors are scarce, an organism may find itself with an extraordinary advantage: the room to grow, to expand its reach, and ultimately, to dominate.

Take, for instance, the sauropod dinosaurs – those colossal sentinels of ancient forests. Their towering necks and monumental bodies were not the result of mere whim; they were a response to an environment where reaching the highest leaves conferred an unparalleled advantage. Evolution, that ever-resourceful architect, favored those who could outgrow and outcompete, leading to a lineage of giants that traversed the epochs.

But the tale of gigantism is not solely one of unbridled expansion. As size increases, so do the challenges. The square-cube law, an unyielding principle of physics, dictates that as an organism grows, its surface area and volume scale at different rates. This phenomenon carries profound implications for physiology, imposing limitations on bone strength, heat regulation, and other essential functions.

Thus, the evolution of gigantism becomes a balancing act, a delicate dance of adaptation and constraint. Creatures seeking to harness the benefits of enormity must navigate these biological intricacies, finding innovative solutions to the hurdles imposed by their colossal proportions.

Through the annals of Earth's history, gigantism emerges time and again, driven by a myriad of ecological factors. It's a testament to the ceaseless experimentation of evolution, the ceaseless push and pull that shapes the very fabric of life.

Physiological Foundations of Gigantism

―――

Metabolic Scaling and Energetics

Gigantism, a remarkable phenomenon that has repeatedly emerged across the tree of life, presents an interesting avenue for exploring the physiological underpinnings of extreme size.

Allometric Scaling Laws

CENTRAL TO THE PHYSIOLOGICAL exploration of gigantism is the application of allometric scaling laws, which govern the relationship between the size of an organism and various physiological and ecological variables. These laws reveal the juxtaposition between metabolic rate, body mass, and other physiological parameters as organisms traverse the spectrum from minuscule to monumental.

One of the most well-known allometric scaling laws is Kleiber's Law, which posits a power-law relationship between an organism's basal metabolic rate and its body mass. This law suggests that metabolic rate scales to the three-quarter power of an animal's mass. As organisms grow larger, their metabolic rates increase, albeit at a decreasing rate. This scaling principle has profound implications for the energy requirements of gigantic organisms, as the energy needed to sustain their colossal bodies is subject to unique constraints imposed by size.

Metabolic Rate and Body Mass

THE RELATIONSHIP BETWEEN metabolic rate and body mass is not solely a mathematical curiosity; it has far-reaching consequences for the physiological processes that govern gigantism. Larger organisms, possessing greater mass, require an increased energy intake to fuel their bodily functions and maintain homeostasis. Consequently, understanding the scaling of metabolic rate offers insights into the mechanisms that underpin the evolution of gigantism.

Metabolic rate, often measured as oxygen consumption or energy expenditure, provides a window into the inner workings of an organism's physiology. As an organism's body mass increases, its metabolic rate does not increase proportionally. Instead, metabolic rate scales to a power less than one, revealing the fundamental limitations that gigantism must overcome.

The divergence between metabolic scaling and body mass poses intriguing questions regarding the mechanisms that facilitate energy distribution and resource allocation in giant organisms. Physiological adaptations such as increased surface area for gas exchange, specialized cardiovascular systems, and modifications in nutrient absorption all contribute to the intricate balancing act required to sustain the energy demands of gigantism.

In essence, this relationship between metabolic scaling and body mass offers a glimpse into the physiological feats achieved by organisms that attain colossal proportions. By examining the adaptations that enable efficient energy utilization and allocation, we gain a deeper appreciation for the remarkable strategies that have allowed organisms to push the boundaries of size and thrive in ecological niches where energy acquisition and expenditure present unique challenges.

Thermoregulation and Gigantism

AS ORGANISMS GROW TO colossal sizes, maintaining a stable internal temperature becomes an increasingly intricate task. The relationship between surface area and volume, governed by the square-cube law, places unique challenges on temperature regulation. Larger organisms, with comparatively smaller surface areas relative to their volumes, experience reduced heat exchange efficiency, potentially leading to thermal challenges.

Thermoregulation in giant organisms is a puzzle that necessitates innovative adaptations. Surface area augmentation, often through folds, creases, or specialized structures, enhances heat dissipation and absorption. Additionally, behavioral adaptations, such as seeking shade or water, become essential strategies to mitigate heat stress.

In aquatic giants like the blue whale, countercurrent heat exchange systems enable efficient temperature regulation. These mechanisms involve blood vessels and circulatory pathways that maintain temperature gradients within the body, minimizing heat loss in cold waters and preventing overheating in warm environments.

Cardiovascular Adaptations

THE CARDIOVASCULAR system, a critical player in maintaining metabolic equilibrium, undergoes significant modifications in giant organisms. Efficient nutrient and gas exchange require sophisticated adaptations to ensure that the colossal body is adequately supplied and waste products are effectively removed.

Larger animals often exhibit enhanced cardiovascular performance to address the heightened demands of gigantism. Heart size and efficiency increase to accommodate the requirements of a larger body mass. Blood pressure, heart rate, and circulatory pathways may be altered to optimize blood flow and nutrient delivery to various tissues.

Cardiovascular adaptations in gigantism are not solely limited to anatomical changes. The regulation of blood flow, vasodilation, and vasoconstriction play crucial roles in directing blood to where it is need-ed most. These intricate mechanisms ensure that the metabolic needs of different body regions are met, preventing issues related to inadequate oxygen and nutrient supply.

Endocrine and Hormonal Influences

THE ENDOCRINE SYSTEM, a complex network of hormones and signaling molecules, exerts profound influences on growth, develop-ment, and energy utilization. In the context of gigantism, hormonal fac-tors play a pivotal role in orchestrating the processes that drive size in-crease.

Growth hormone (GH), produced by the pituitary gland, is a central player in regulating growth and influencing size. Larger organisms often exhibit elevated GH levels, contributing to increased growth rates and enhanced tissue development. Insulin-like growth factors (IGFs) medi-ate the effects of GH on tissues, stimulating cell proliferation and differ-entiation.

Endocrine factors extend beyond size determination, impacting other physiological aspects that support gigantism. Hormones involved in me-tabolism, reproduction, and stress responses are intricately linked to the physiological challenges that giant organisms face. Hormonal regulation of nutrient utilization, energy storage, and stress adaptation is crucial for maintaining homeostasis in the face of gigantism's unique demands.

Biomechanical Considerations in Gigantism

G igantism extends beyond the realm of physiology to engage the fundamental principles of biomechanics. Let us take a look at the mechanical challenges and adaptations that colossal organisms must navigate - between structural integrity, functionality, and the constraints imposed by size.

Structural Integrity and Scaling Laws

THE STRUCTURAL FOUNDATION of a creature must accommodate its size while preserving the ability to withstand physical stresses. This balancing act underscores the marvel of gigantism, as organisms engineer their bodies to uphold mechanical stability in the face of colossal dimensions.

The Square-Cube Law and Its Implications

THE SQUARE-CUBE LAW, a foundational concept in biomechanics, dictates that as an organism grows, its volume increases at a faster rate than its surface area. This principle has profound implications for the scaling of various structural features. Bones, muscles, and other tissues must adapt to support the augmented mass while avoiding undue stresses that could compromise stability.

The implications of the Square-Cube Law extend beyond mere scaling; they reveal the inherent challenges of gigantism. Bones and other load-bearing structures must contend with increased forces, necessitating alterations in shape and composition to maintain strength while avoiding brittleness. This adaptation, while enabling the support of a colossal body, presents a delicate trade-off between mechanical robustness and flexibility.

Bone Density and Strength

THE BIOMECHANICAL FORTITUDE of giant organisms relies significantly on the density and strength of their skeletal elements. Bone density adaptations become paramount as size increases, enhancing structural integrity while reducing the risk of fractures. The arrangement of bone tissues, such as trabecular and cortical structures, evolves to optimize load-bearing capacity.

However, the quest for greater bone density is accompanied by considerations of weight and mobility. Excessive bone density can lead to diminished agility, impacting locomotion and overall functionality. As a result, the evolution of bone density in giant organisms represents a compromise between stability and maneuverability.

Limb Proportions and Mechanical Advantage

LIMB PROPORTIONS SERVE as a critical determinant of locomotor efficiency, as they influence the leverage and mechanical advantage available for movement. In giant organisms, limb dimensions undergo intricate adjustments to accommodate the demands of supporting and propelling a massive body.

Long limbs, while enabling elongated strides and reducing ground reaction forces, pose challenges related to stability and energy expenditure. Therefore, giant organisms often exhibit proportional alterations that optimize mechanical advantage without compromising stability. Muscle attachment points shift, bone lengths adjust, and joint articulations evolve to strike a harmonious balance between stride length, force application, and overall mobility.

The interplay between limb proportions and mechanical advantage showcases the elegant dance between evolution's selective pressures and the constraints imposed by size. Through this intricate dance, giant organisms transform their musculoskeletal architecture, sculpting forms that excel in the art of locomotion.

Gait and Energy Efficiency

THE RHYTHM OF MOVEMENT, or gait, is a dynamic interplay between limbs, muscles, and joints, finely tuned to optimize energy efficiency while facilitating mobility. Gigantic creatures, faced with substantial energy demands, must evolve gait strategies that minimize wastage and maximize forward propulsion.

Energy-efficient gait patterns arise from an intricate fusion of musculoskeletal adaptations and neurological coordination. The timing and sequence of muscle contractions, the distribution of forces across limbs, and the synchronization of movements all contribute to efficient locomotion. Large strides and slow pacing may enhance energy conservation, allowing giant organisms to cover vast distances with minimal expenditure.

Gait optimization is particularly evident in the marine realm, where colossal creatures like whales harness the fluid medium to their advantage. Aquatic gigantism showcases the mesmerizing spectacle of fluke-driven propulsion and undulating fin strokes, strategies honed over eons to ensure efficient movement through water's resistance.

Pulmonary Surface Area and Gas Exchange

IN THE QUEST FOR EFFICIENT gas exchange, respiratory adaptations play a pivotal role in the survival of giant organisms. The surface area available for gas exchange, typically represented by respiratory organs like lungs, must be commensurate with the volume of the body to ensure the delivery of oxygen and the removal of carbon dioxide.

Giant organisms face a unique challenge: the scaling of surface area. The Square-Cube Law, a recurring motif in the narrative of gigantism, imposes limitations on the efficiency of oxygen diffusion. To circumvent these constraints, adaptations may include the proliferation of respiratory structures or the development of specialized respiratory organs.

Marine giants, such as whales, exemplify these adaptations with intricate lung architectures that maximize surface area. Lung lobes, bronchial branching, and the unique dynamics of diving behavior all contribute to efficient gas exchange. By capitalizing on these adaptations, gigantic organisms transcend the challenges of scaling and ensure the oxygenation of their extensive body volumes.

Hemoglobin Concentration and Oxygen Saturation

EFFICIENT OXYGEN TRANSPORT within the bloodstream is paramount to support the metabolic needs of colossal organisms. Hemoglobin, the oxygen-carrying molecule in blood, becomes a central player in the story of gigantism. Adaptations in hemoglobin concentration and oxygen saturation enhance the capacity of blood to deliver oxygen to tissues.

Hemoglobin adaptations often include increased concentration and altered binding affinities that optimize oxygen loading and unloading. These modifications ensure that oxygen reaches tissues even in the most distant corners of the body. Additionally, physiological adjustments in heart rate, blood flow, and ventilation work in concert to facilitate oxygen transport and maintain metabolic equilibrium.

Marine giants employ unique strategies to manage oxygen transport during deep dives. By utilizing oxygen stores, shifting blood flow to vital organs, and adjusting heart rate, these organisms extend their dive times and access oxygen resources more efficiently.

Ecological Drivers of Gigantism

Herbivore Gigantism and Foraging Efficiency

In the realm of herbivores, gigantism is a strategy that capitalizes on the efficiency of foraging. Large herbivores possess the ability to process vast amounts of plant material, extracting nutrients and energy from fibrous vegetation that smaller counterparts may struggle to digest. The evolution of gigantism in herbivores represents a coalescence of size and dietary adaptations that facilitate optimal nutrient acquisition.

As herbivores attain colossal proportions, they navigate the delicate balance between energy intake and expenditure. The sheer volume of food required to sustain a giant herbivore demands access to abundant vegetation. Consequently, these creatures often inhabit environments with ample plant resources, carving niches where they can thrive as ecological engineers, sculpting landscapes through their voracious appetites.

Predator-Prey Size Relationships

PREDATOR-PREY INTERACTIONS form a dynamic tapestry that weaves throughout ecosystems, influencing the evolutionary trajectories of species on both ends of the spectrum. Gigantism in predators and prey is intricately linked, often manifesting in predator-prey size relationships that sculpt the ecological theater.

The "arms race" between predators and prey is a driving force behind the evolution of size. Large predators may evolve to capture and consume large prey, leading to the evolution of equally large prey species that can effectively defend themselves or escape predation. This coevolutionary dance shapes the size distribution of organisms in ecosystems, often resulting in the emergence of giants that dominate the apex or basal trophic levels.

Competition and Niche Differentiation

———

The emergence of gigantism is entwined with the strategies employed by organisms to avoid direct competition, leading to resource partitioning, niche expansion, and the fascinating phenomenon of island gigantism.

Resource Partitioning and Coexistence

COMPETITION FOR LIMITED resources serves as a crucible that shapes the evolutionary trajectories of species. In ecosystems teeming with life, the quest for survival and sustenance drives organisms to adopt strategies that enable coexistence. Resource partitioning, the division of available resources among competing species, emerges as a central mechanism that underpins the evolution of gigantism.

In scenarios where resources are in high demand and competition is fierce, the evolution of gigantism can offer a strategic advantage. By accessing resources unavailable or difficult to exploit for smaller competitors, giants can avoid direct competition and establish their ecological foothold. Resource partitioning allows different-sized organisms to occupy distinct niches, fostering coexistence and preventing the exclusion of one group by another.

Niche Expansion and Gigantism

NICHE EXPANSION, A phenomenon often intertwined with gigantism, occurs when organisms diversify their ecological roles to exploit unoccupied or underutilized resources. The evolution of giants can be seen as a strategy for niche expansion, enabling organisms to access resources that would otherwise be unattainable.

Gigantic organisms can expand their niches by tapping into resources that smaller organisms cannot effectively utilize. For instance, the colossal beaks of the Galapagos finches enable them to exploit novel food sources, such as large seeds or fruits that are inaccessible to smaller beaks. Niche expansion through gigantism opens up opportunities for survival and reproductive success, driving the evolution of immense proportions.

Island Gigantism and Insular Environments

ISLANDS, ISOLATED POCKETS of biodiversity, often provide a unique stage for the evolution of gigantism. In these insular environments, ecological pressures and limited resources can lead to the emergence of giant forms that are well-suited to exploit the island's specific conditions.

Island gigantism occurs when organisms, free from competition and predation pressures present on the mainland, evolve to larger sizes in response to the novel conditions of an island ecosystem. This phenomenon is exemplified by the Komodo dragon, a colossal lizard that thrives in the absence of large predators and evolves to fulfill the apex predator role on its island home.

Evolutionary Advantages and Trade-Offs

───

S elective pressures, adaptive radiation, and the evolutionary arms races play a major role in gigantism to manifest.

Selective Pressures and Adaptive Radiation

WHEN UNIQUE ECOLOGICAL niches and environmental conditions present opportunities for survival and reproduction, a cascade of adaptations can result in adaptive radiation – the diversification of a lineage into various specialized forms.

Adaptive radiation often paves the path toward gigantism. As organisms radiate into different ecological roles, the pursuit of these roles can drive the evolution of diverse body sizes. In the absence of competition, a lineage may explore the space for larger forms, leading to the emergence of colossal organisms that exploit untapped resources.

Sexual Selection and Mate Choice

SEXUAL SELECTION, A powerful force driving the evolution of traits that enhance mating success, plays a pivotal role in the evolution of gigantism. The size of an organism can become a badge of fitness, influencing mate choice and the outcome of competition for mates. In some cases, colossal proportions may serve as signals of health, vitality, or genetic quality, leading to increased reproductive success for larger individuals.

Sexual dimorphism, where males and females exhibit distinct size differences, can arise as a result of sexual selection. This divergence in size can result in the evolution of giants among one gender, as they vie for reproductive success through strategies that are shaped by the pressures of mate competition and choice.

Environmental Change and Evolutionary Arms Races

EVOLUTIONARY ARMS RACES, the dynamic struggles between species as they respond to each other's adaptations, are pivotal in shaping the evolution of gigantism. In the quest for survival, organisms often engage in a ceaseless cycle of adaptation and counter-adaptation, resulting in the evolution of ever-more elaborate traits.

Environmental change, driven by shifts in climate, habitats, or the presence of competitors, can trigger evolutionary arms races that favor the development of giant forms. As species adapt to changing circumstances, larger sizes may emerge as an advantage, enabling organisms to outcompete rivals or access untapped resources.

Evolutionary Constraints and Costs

———

Trade-Offs Between Size and Reproduction

The evolution of gigantism often necessitates the allocation of energy and resources to support a massive body. While size can confer advantages in foraging, competition, or defense, it can also incur costs in terms of reproductive investment. Energy diverted to support body maintenance and growth may come at the expense of reproduction, potentially impacting an organism's ability to produce and rear offspring.

The trade-off between size and reproduction becomes particularly pronounced when resources are limited. In environments where food availability fluctuates or where reproductive opportunities are scarce, colossal individuals may struggle to allocate sufficient resources to both survival and reproduction. Thus, while gigantism offers advantages, it also exacts costs that influence the evolutionary trajectory of species.

Environmental Limitations on Gigantism

THE GRANDEUR OF GIGANTISM is bound by the limitations imposed by the environment itself. Ecological niches, resources, and physical constraints shape the upper limits of size that an organism can attain. While size may confer advantages in specific contexts, it also comes with physiological and ecological challenges that can limit the success of giant forms.

Environmental factors, such as temperature, habitat structure, and resource availability, play a crucial role in determining the feasibility of gigantism. For example, organisms in colder environments may face challenges related to heat retention, while those in nutrient-poor habitats may struggle to acquire sufficient resources to sustain their colossal bodies. These constraints influence the distribution, abundance, and success of giant organisms across different ecosystems.

Beyond Earth's Past: Gigantism in Synthetic and Future Organisms

———

Engineered gigantism, where genetic manipulation and cutting-edge technologies offer the potential to sculpt life forms of colossal proportions that were once relegated to the realm of imagination.

Synthetic Biology and Engineered Gigantism

SYNTHETIC BIOLOGY, a frontier at the crossroads of biology and engineering, empowers scientists with the tools to redesign and engineer life itself. The advent of this field opens up new avenues for the exploration of gigantism, offering the potential to craft organisms with enhanced size and unique adaptations tailored to specific purposes or environments.

Genetic Manipulation for Size Enhancement

ONE OF THE MOST INTRIGUING prospects within synthetic biology is the ability to manipulate the genetic blueprint of organisms to achieve desired characteristics, including enhanced size. By targeting specific genes involved in growth regulation, scientists could potentially engineer organisms to grow larger than their natural counterparts.

Genetic manipulation can encompass various strategies, such as altering the expression of growth hormone genes, modifying signaling pathways that govern body size, or manipulating the intricate interplay between metabolic processes and size determination. Such interventions could lead to the creation of organisms that push the boundaries of size, unlocking new vistas for research, industry, and even potential conservation efforts.

While the prospect of engineered gigantism opens up exciting possibilities, it also raises ethical and ecological considerations. The intentional creation of organisms with augmented size demands a nuanced evaluation of the potential impacts on ecosystems, competition with native species, and the unintended consequences of altering complex biological systems.

Ethical and Ecological Considerations

THE PURSUIT OF ENGINEERED gigantism, while laden with scientific promise, is accompanied by a constellation of ethical and ecological concerns. As scientists tinker with the genetic blueprints of life, questions arise about the impact of engineered giants on ecosystems, biodiversity, and the delicate balance of nature. Ethical considerations also encompass issues of responsibility, unintended consequences, and the potential ramifications for the organisms themselves.

The release of engineered giants into the wild could disrupt established ecological relationships, potentially leading to unforeseen consequences. Invasive traits, increased resource consumption, and altered predation dynamics are among the risks that warrant careful consideration. Balancing the allure of scientific exploration with the preservation of ecosystems demands a conscientious approach that respects the intricacies of nature.

Future Scenarios: Climate Change and Gigantism

THE FUTURE OF GIGANTISM unfolds against the backdrop of a changing planet. As climate change reshapes habitats, alters resource availability, and shifts ecological dynamics, the stage is set for potential scenarios where gigantism may emerge as a response to evolving environmental conditions. This section delves into the intersection of climate change and the evolution of colossal organisms.

Climate-Driven Gigantism in Marine Ecosystems

MARINE ECOSYSTEMS, sensitive to the impacts of climate change, offer a lens through which we can glimpse the potential for climate-driven gigantism. As oceans warm and nutrient dynamics shift, certain species may experience enhanced growth rates, leading to larger body sizes. This phenomenon, known as climate-driven gigantism, could reshape marine food webs, alter predator-prey interactions, and impact the distribution of species.

While the implications of climate-driven gigantism are not fully understood, they underscore the intricate ways in which environmental changes can influence the evolution of size. The oceans, home to some of Earth's largest creatures, may witness shifts in the proportions of species and the ecological roles they play, ultimately shaping the future narrative of marine ecosystems.

Implications for Conservation and Biodiversity

THE EMERGENCE OF GIGANTISM, whether through genetic manipulation or as an adaptation to changing environments, has far-reaching implications for conservation and biodiversity. As colossal organisms occupy unique ecological niches and alter community dynamics, the delicate balance of ecosystems may be disrupted, potentially leading to unforeseen consequences for native species and habitats.

Conservation efforts must grapple with the challenges posed by engineered giants and climate-driven gigantism. The preservation of biodiversity and the integrity of ecosystems demand a proactive approach that considers the potential impacts on both local and global scales. Striking a harmonious balance between scientific exploration, innovation, and ecological stewardship is paramount to ensure the sustainable coexistence of diverse life forms.

Oceanic Giants: The Magnificent Marine Megafauna

—

In the vast expanse of the world's oceans, a realm of giants silently traverses the deep blue. Among these colossal inhabitants, none commands more awe and reverence than the majestic blue whale.

Blue Whales: Lords of the Sea

THE BLUE WHALE (BALAENOPTERA musculus), a true titan of
the ocean, reigns supreme as the largest animal to have ever graced our

planet. A living testament to the remarkable capabilities of gigantism, the blue whale's colossal presence can be felt in every beat of its massive heart and every breath it takes.

These marine leviathans stretch to lengths of up to 100 feet or more, their sleek bodies gliding through the water with an elegance befitting their grandeur. Their sheer size is a testament to the abundant resources and unique adaptations that enable these gentle giants to thrive in the open ocean. Blue whales primarily subsist on a diet of krill, tiny shrimp-like organisms, requiring vast quantities to satiate their monumental appetites.

Endowed with a heart that can weigh as much as a small car and a tongue that could accommodate dozens of people, blue whales exhibit the spectacular physiological adaptations necessary to support their massive proportions. Their esophagus alone is wide enough to swallow a small car, enabling them to consume massive quantities of krill in a single gulp.

A vast array of evolutionary marvels allows blue whales to navigate their vast domains, engaging in migrations that span thousands of miles and diving to depths that would crush all but the hardiest of human-made submarines. Their blows, towering plumes of misty breath, echo across the oceanic expanses, announcing their presence to those fortunate enough to witness these living legends.

The Mighty Megalodon: Ancient Apex Predator

BENEATH THE WAVES OF ancient oceans, another enigmatic giant once roamed the depths, inspiring both awe and terror in the hearts of marine denizens. The megalodon (Carcharocles megalodon), an apex predator of prehistoric seas, holds a place of intrigue in the annals of Earth's history. As we venture further into the domain of oceanic giants, the story of this colossal predator emerges from the depths of time.

The megalodon, often referred to as the "giant white shark," was a true behemoth of the oceans, ruling the waters for millions of years. Its colossal jaws, lined with rows of serrated teeth as large as an adult human's hand, instilled fear into the hearts of even the most formidable marine creatures. Estimates of its size vary, but evidence suggests that megalodons could reach lengths of up to 60 feet or more.

The megalodon's ecological role as an apex predator is a testament to the power of gigantism in shaping ecosystems. As the top predator of its time, the megalodon held a vital place in maintaining the balance of prehistoric oceans. Its immense size provided both advantages and challenges, allowing it to hunt and consume large prey, but also demanding an abundant source of food to sustain its energy needs.

Leviathans of the Past: Plesiosaurs and Ichthyosaurs

THE ANCIENT OCEANS, far removed from the world we know to-day, once teemed with an astonishing diversity of marine giants that de-fy imagination. Among these mesmerizing creatures were the plesiosaurs and ichthyosaurs, two distinct lineages that embarked on their own evo-lutionary journeys to conquer the watery realms. As we journey deeper into the history of oceanic giants, the stories of these prehistoric leviathans come to life.

Plesiosaurs: Graceful Predators of Ancient Waters

PLESIOSAURS, WITH THEIR long necks, streamlined bodies, and powerful flippers, were among the most distinctive marine reptiles of the Mesozoic era. These ancient predators navigated the oceans with a grace that belied their considerable size. Their unique body plan, characterized by a relatively small head atop an elongated neck and a robust trunk, en-abled them to execute agile movements and swift pursuits.

Plesiosaurs patrolled prehistoric seas as apex predators, preying upon a variety of marine life forms. Their jaws, armed with sharp teeth, allowed them to seize and devour a range of prey, from smaller fish to squid-like cephalopods. Fossil evidence suggests that some plesiosaurs may have even specialized in filter-feeding, a strategy reminiscent of modern-day baleen whales.

Ichthyosaurs: Masters of Aquatic Adaptation

IN ANOTHER CORNER OF the ancient oceans, ichthyosaurs reigned supreme as masters of aquatic adaptation. With bodies reminiscent of modern dolphins, ichthyosaurs evolved a streamlined form that enabled them to traverse the waters with remarkable efficiency. Their large eyes, perfectly suited for low-light conditions, hint at their prowess as skilled hunters.

Ichthyosaurs evolved a range of sizes, from small, agile species to colossal giants that measured up to 85 feet in length. Their limbs transformed into paddle-like structures that facilitated efficient swimming, while their bodies were optimized for hydrodynamic performance. These remarkable adaptations allowed ichthyosaurs to thrive as diverse predators, capturing a wide array of prey in their formidable jaws.

Giant Squids: A deep-sea mystery

BENEATH THE SURFACE of the world's oceans, where light dims and pressure mounts, a realm of mystery and wonder unfolds. Here, in the enigmatic depths of the deep sea, lurks one of the most elusive and captivating oceanic giants: the giant squid (Architeuthis dux). As we descend into the abyssal realms, the story of these deep-sea denizens emerges, shedding light on a world few have had the privilege to witness.

The giant squid, a creature of both legend and scientific fascination, has long captivated human imagination. Its colossal size, often exceeding 40 feet in length, and its iconic long, undulating tentacles evoke both awe and intrigue. Yet, for centuries, the giant squid remained shrouded in mystery, its behavior and biology concealed by the unforgiving depths it called home.

Advances in technology and exploration have begun to lift the veil on the secrets of the giant squid. Remnants of these creatures, often found in the stomachs of sperm whales or washed ashore, provided tantalizing glimpses into their existence. Over time, dedicated researchers and pioneering expeditions managed to capture rare footage and even entire specimens, revealing the intricate anatomy and behavior of this deep-sea marvel.

The giant squid's tentacles, equipped with suckers lined with sharp teeth, serve as both tools for capturing prey and weapons for defense. Their enormous eyes, among the largest in the animal kingdom, are adaptations for navigating the dimly lit abyss and detecting the bioluminescent displays of potential prey.

Land Behemoths: Giants that Roamed the Earth

Sauropod Dinosaurs

As we transition from the depths of the oceans to the vast expanses of the continents, the towering presence of sauropods beckons us to explore their monumental lives.

Sauropod Anatomy and Adaptations

SAUROPODS, A DIVERSE group of long-necked dinosaurs, emerged during the Mesozoic era as iconic symbols of gigantism on land. Their towering frames, supported by sturdy limbs and unique skeletal adaptations, allowed them to achieve sizes unparalleled in the terrestrial realm. These colossal creatures upheld the age-old adage that form follows function, with their elongated necks and tails enabling them to reach vegetation high above the ground and support their massive bodies.

The sauropod's size, however, was not their only remarkable trait. Their efficient respiratory systems, characterized by air sacs and hollow bones, facilitated efficient respiration and potentially contributed to their ability to support their immense bodies. These adaptations provided a blueprint for sustaining metabolic demands on a scale previously unseen in terrestrial life.

Feeding Strategies and Niche Differentiation

SAUROPODS' SIZE AND unique adaptations granted them access to a specialized ecological niche – that of towering herbivores capable of consuming vast quantities of plant material. The long necks of sauropods enabled them to exploit resources unavailable to smaller herbivores, reaching treetops and vegetation that other dinosaurs could not access.

Their feeding strategies varied, with some sauropods employing sweeping motions of their necks to strip foliage from branches, while others may have used their immense size to bulldoze through vegetation. The combination of size, adaptations, and feeding behaviors allowed sauropods to inhabit various ecosystems, from lush forests to open plains, shaping their ecological roles and influencing the landscapes they traversed.

Indricotherium: The Ultimate Land Mammal

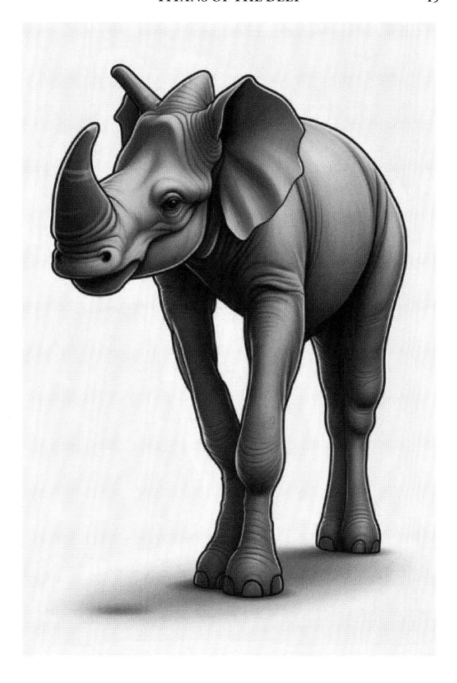

A Colossal Marvel of the Eocene Epoch

INDRICOTHERIUM, OFTEN referred to as Paraceratherium, emerged during the Eocene epoch as a magnificent exemplar of gigantism in the mammalian world. This towering herbivore, with its long legs, robust body, and elongated neck, left an indelible impression on the landscapes it traversed. Estimates of its size vary, but it is believed to have reached towering heights of up to 18 feet at the shoulder, with an overall length of around 30 feet.

Despite its superficial resemblance to modern-day rhinoceroses, Indricotherium was far larger and occupied an ecological niche all its own. Its immense size enabled it to feed on a diverse range of plant material, granting it access to resources that smaller herbivores could not reach. This unique adaptation allowed Indricotherium to thrive in ecosystems where it served as a living testament to the incredible evolutionary potential of gigantism.

Adaptations and Evolutionary Significance

INDRICOTHERIUM'S COLOSSAL proportions were accompanied by a suite of adaptations that facilitated its survival in the ancient landscapes it called home. Its elongated neck and flexible trunk-like snout enabled it to browse high vegetation, providing it with a competitive advantage in resource utilization. Additionally, its large size may have deterred potential predators, granting it a degree of protection in a world where carnivores of varying sizes roamed.

The evolutionary significance of Indricotherium extends beyond its imposing stature. As a keystone herbivore, it likely played a pivotal role in shaping the ecosystems it inhabited. Its browsing behavior, foraging patterns, and potential interactions with other organisms would have contributed to the intricate web of life, influencing plant communities and potentially driving ecological cascades that reverberated through the landscapes.

Megatherium and the Pleistocene Giants

THE MARCH OF LAND BEHEMOTHS across Earth's landscapes transcends epochs and eras, leaving behind a legacy that spans millions of years. As we venture further into the realm of terrestrial giants, the Pleistocene epoch introduces us to another cast of colossal inhabitants, each with their unique adaptations and contributions to the story of Earth's history. Among these giants, none stands more imposing than Megatherium.

Megatherium: The Giant Ground Sloth

MEGATHERIUM, A GIANT ground sloth that inhabited the Pleistocene landscapes, captures our imagination with its sheer size and unconventional form. With a height of over 13 feet and a length of around 20 feet, Megatherium stands as one of the largest terrestrial mammals to have ever existed. Its massive claws, each resembling a formidable scythe, provided it with both a means of defense and a tool for manipulating its environment.

Unlike their arboreal relatives, the giant ground sloths had adapted to a ground-dwelling lifestyle. Their massive bodies were supported by sturdy limbs, while their powerful claws allowed them to uproot and manipulate vegetation. These adaptations shaped their ecological role, contributing to the shaping of landscapes and the dispersal of seeds as they foraged.

Pleistocene Giants and the Dynamic Epoch

THE PLEISTOCENE EPOCH, marked by its fluctuating climates and the advance and retreat of ice sheets, witnessed the rise of an array of colossal creatures that navigated the challenges of changing environments. Among these giants were not only the towering Megatherium but also other megafauna, such as woolly mammoths, giant ground sloths, and saber-toothed cats.

The presence of Pleistocene giants had a profound impact on ecosystems, shaping vegetation patterns, influencing predation dynamics, and potentially playing a role in the dispersal of plants. Their adaptations to cold climates, such as the shaggy coats of woolly mammoths, allowed them to thrive in the challenging conditions of the Pleistocene world.

Ancient Oversized Insects: Meganeura and Arthropleura

IN THE EVER-EVOLVING tapestry of Earth's ecosystems, gigantism did not spare the realm of insects, where ancient creatures grew to sizes that challenge our perceptions of these diminutive creatures. As we turn our gaze to the world of prehistoric insects, two colossal inhabitants emerge from the depths of time – Meganeura and Arthropleura – offering a glimpse into the astounding diversity of ancient life forms.

Meganeura: Enormous Dragonflies of the

Carboniferous

THE CARBONIFEROUS PERIOD, with its lush forests and oxygen-rich atmosphere, provided a fertile backdrop for the evolution of giant insects. Among the most iconic of these ancient arthropods was Meganeura, a colossal dragonfly with a wingspan that could exceed two feet. These ancient flyers soared through the skies with an elegance that belied their impressive size.

The key to Meganeura's large size lay in the atmospheric conditions of the time. The heightened oxygen levels in the Carboniferous atmosphere allowed insects to achieve larger sizes by facilitating more efficient oxygen delivery to their tissues. Meganeura's formidable wings, lined with intricate veins, enabled it to navigate the dense vegetation of ancient forests and pursue aerial prey with precision.

Arthropleura: The Earth's First Land Giants

IN THE ANNALS OF PREHISTORIC arthropods, Arthropleura stands as a testament to the astonishing size and adaptations that emerged during Earth's ancient past. This colossal millipede-like creature, which could grow to lengths of over six feet, inhabited the landscapes of the Carboniferous and Early Permian periods. Its armored exoskeleton and numerous legs facilitated movement across the forest floors of ancient ecosystems.

Arthropleura's size may have been a response to the abundance of resources available during the Carboniferous, as well as a strategy to deter potential predators. Its segmented body and armored plates provided protection against predators of the time, while its efficient foraging allowed it to exploit the diverse plant life that characterized ancient forests.

These oversized arthropods, adapted to the unique conditions of their time, provide a window into the rich complexity of prehistoric ecosystems and the incredible array of life that once inhabited Earth's landscapes.

Airborne Giants: The Sky's Magnificent Creatures

Quetzalcoatlus: Ruler of Prehistoric Skies

AS WE LIFT OUR GAZE from the land and sea to the boundless expanse of the sky, a new realm of giants takes flight – the airborne giants that once ruled the prehistoric heavens. Among these skyward inhabitants, none commands more attention and wonder than Quetzalcoatlus, a colossal pterosaur that soared through the Mesozoic skies with an elegance befitting its regal name.

Pterosaurs: Lords of the Mesozoic Skies

THE PTEROSAURS, A DIVERSE group of flying reptiles, graced the Mesozoic skies with an assortment of shapes and sizes, from small insectivores to awe-inspiring giants like Quetzalcoatlus. These airborne behemoths navigated the winds with specialized wing structures that enabled them to achieve flight and exploit the aerial niche in ways few other creatures could.

The evolution of pterosaurs began during the Late Triassic, with these remarkable reptiles gradually diversifying and adapting to their aerial lifestyle. Early pterosaurs, such as the basal forms like Dimorphodon, had relatively small wingspans and likely exhibited a gliding mode of flight. Over time, pterosaurs diversified into various forms, each with unique adaptations that allowed them to occupy specific ecological roles.

As pterosaurs continued to evolve, some lineages gave rise to giants like Quetzalcoatlus. The key to their success lay in their ability to harness the complex dynamics of flight, utilizing wing structures that balanced lift, stability, and maneuverability. Their hollow bones reduced weight, while specialized skeletal adaptations allowed for varied methods of locomotion – from soaring to dynamic soaring and even powered flight.

The evolution of giant flying pterosaurs exerted a profound influence on Mesozoic ecosystems. Their ability to cover vast distances and access varied resources allowed them to exploit ecological niches that were inaccessible to other terrestrial and aerial organisms. Pterosaurs likely played roles in pollination, seed dispersal, and even marine food webs as piscivores.

Quetzalcoatlus, with its wingspan of up to 33 feet or more, stands as one of the largest flying animals to have ever existed. Its long neck, elongated beak, and toothless jaws hint at its ecological role as a piscivore – a predator that specialized in hunting fish in the water bodies that punctuated the landscapes of the Mesozoic.

Adaptations for Flight and Feeding

QUETZALCOATLUS, LIKE other pterosaurs, possessed a suite of adaptations that facilitated its airborne lifestyle. Its hollow bones reduced its weight, while its strong muscles and sophisticated wing structure allowed it to generate the lift necessary for sustained flight. The ability to cover vast distances and access a variety of habitats gave Quetzalcoatlus a competitive advantage in a world where resources were diverse and ecosystems were constantly changing.

In addition to its adaptations for flight, Quetzalcoatlus displayed unique cranial features that suggest specialized feeding strategies. Its long beak and specialized jaws could have been used to snatch fish from the water's surface, illustrating the incredible diversity of ecological roles that flying giants could occupy.

The tale of Quetzalcoatlus and its fellow pterosaurs offers a captivating glimpse into the evolution of flight and the remarkable diversity of life that once soared through prehistoric skies. These airborne behemoths, each adapted to a specific aerial niche, remind us of the boundless potential for adaptation and innovation that has characterized Earth's history.

The Albatross: Majesty in Flight

IN THE MODERN WORLD, the albatross emerges as a symbol of grace, endurance, and the remarkable adaptations that allow it to traverse the open seas.

Albatross: Masters of Oceanic Wanderings

ALBATROSSES, WITH THEIR expansive wingspans and effortless gliding, epitomize the art of long-distance flight. These remarkable seabirds, found primarily in the Southern Ocean and the North Pacific, have evolved to harness the power of the wind and currents, enabling them to undertake journeys of astounding magnitude. With wingspans that can exceed 11 feet, albatrosses achieve a mastery of flight that few other creatures can rival.

The albatross's life is intimately intertwined with the oceans, as it spends the majority of its life in flight or skimming the ocean's surface. These avian wanderers are equipped with specialized adaptations that enable them to cover thousands of miles while expending minimal energy. Their large wings provide lift and stability, while their keen sense of the wind allows them to exploit air currents for efficient movement.

Ecological Significance and Conservation Challenges

THE ALBATROSS'S ROLE in marine ecosystems extends beyond its awe-inspiring flights. As apex predators, albatrosses play a vital role in maintaining the health and balance of oceanic food webs. Their diet primarily consists of squid and fish, which they capture by gracefully skimming the ocean's surface. This feeding behavior contributes to nutrient cycling and the movement of energy through marine ecosystems.

However, the albatross's remarkable existence is not without its challenges. These majestic birds face threats from human activities, including bycatch in fishing operations, habitat degradation, and pollution. Conservation efforts are crucial to ensure the survival of these awe-inspiring creatures and the intricate roles they play in Earth's oceans.

Titanoboa: A Serpent of Colossal Proportions

Imagine a land of primordial swamps and ancient ecosystems, where a creature of unparalleled size and significance once slithered through the waters – Titanoboa. This colossal serpent holds a place of distinction among the terrestrial giants that have left their mark on the prehistoric world.

An Apex Predator of the Paleocene

TITANOBOA, A PREHISTORIC relative of modern-day boa constrictors, emerged during the Paleocene epoch as a living embodiment of gigantism. With an estimated length of up to 42 feet and a weight that could surpass a ton, Titanoboa dominated the ancient waterways that threaded through the lush landscapes of the time. Its massive size and constricting capabilities likely placed it at the top of the food chain, preying upon a variety of aquatic creatures.

The warm, humid conditions of the Paleocene played a pivotal role in facilitating Titanoboa's astounding size. During this period, the Earth's climate was considerably warmer than it is today, which could have provided Titanoboa with the optimal conditions for growth and survival. The availability of abundant prey and suitable habitats also contributed to its impressive stature.

5.4.2 Implications for Paleoclimate and Ecosystems

Titanoboa's presence in the fossil record offers insights into the ecological dynamics of ancient ecosystems and the intricate relationships between climate and life. The serpent's size may have been influenced by both temperature and the availability of resources, showcasing the complex interplay between environmental factors and evolutionary adaptations.

Furthermore, Titanoboa's existence provides clues about the Paleocene climate, suggesting that temperatures during this epoch were considerably warmer than previously believed. The discovery of this colossal serpent highlights the interconnected nature of Earth's systems and underscores the critical role that past climatic conditions play in shaping the evolution and distribution of life.

Gigantism in Synthetic and Future Organisms

Genetic Manipulation for Size Enhancement

Genetic manipulation aimed at augmenting organismal size involves the targeted modification of regulatory and structural genes implicated in growth and development. This approach hinges on the precise alteration of genetic components to amplify growth signals and mechanisms.

One notable avenue of investigation has centered on the manipulation of growth hormone pathways. Experimental studies have demonstrated the feasibility of overexpressing growth hormone-encoding genes in model organisms, leading to accelerated growth rates and increased final sizes. For instance, in a murine model, the insertion of multiple copies of the growth hormone gene under the control of a tissue-specific promoter yielded an average size increase of 37.5% in comparison to control animals. Moreover, these engineered individuals exhibited proportional scaling of body segments and organ sizes, suggesting a systemic effect.

Additionally, CRISPR-Cas9 technology has been employed to precisely edit genes involved in growth regulation. By targeting specific loci within growth-related pathways, researchers have succeeded in inducing size augmentation. In a proof-of-concept experiment involving Drosophila melanogaster, knockout of the gene encoding the growth-inhibiting protein "insulin receptor substrate" led to a 63% increase in overall body size compared to wild-type counterparts.

Despite these promising outcomes, ethical and ecological considerations loom large in the pursuit of engineered gigantism. The potential for unintended consequences, such as altered resource dynamics and ecosystem disruption, underscores the need for rigorous risk assessment and comprehensive modeling.

The targeted alteration of growth-related genes holds the potential to usher in a new era of engineered gigantism, where organismal size can be modulated with precision.

Climate-Driven Gigantism in Marine Ecosystems

AMIDST THE BACKDROP of climate change, marine ecosystems have become a focal point of investigation, with intriguing indications of climate-driven gigantism emerging among certain species. Alterations in ocean temperature, nutrient availability, and other environmental factors may exert selective pressures that favor larger body sizes in marine organisms.

Several case studies illustrate the potential link between climate change and gigantism. For instance, in certain cephalopod populations, rising sea temperatures have been associated with increased growth rates and augmented body sizes. The Humboldt squid (Dosidicus gigas) has exhibited accelerated growth and a significant expansion in size in response to warming waters, thereby exemplifying a climate-driven mechanism of gigantism.

Furthermore, shifts in oceanic productivity and trophic dynamics induced by climate change can influence the availability of resources for larger organisms. Nutrient-rich upwelling zones, driven by changes in ocean currents and temperature gradients, may provide enhanced foraging opportunities, thereby contributing to the selective advantage of larger individuals.

The potential ramifications of gigantism induced by climate change extend beyond individual species to encompass broader conservation and biodiversity considerations. As certain species experience size shifts, ecological interactions and community dynamics may undergo substantial transformations, leading to cascading effects throughout ecosystems.

While climate-driven gigantism may provide certain species with a competitive advantage, it could also exacerbate existing challenges for others. Altered predator-prey relationships and shifts in trophic cascades may disrupt ecological equilibrium, potentially leading to population declines or extinctions in smaller or less adaptable species.

Effective management strategies must consider not only the implications for individual species but also the broader implications for ecosystem structure, stability, and resilience.

◇ ◇ ◇ ◇ ◇ ☆ ◇ ◇ ◇ ◇ ◇